Raccoons
in the Dark

By Jean Claude O'Mara

Gareth Stevens
Publishing

Please visit our website, www.garethstevens.com. For a free color catalog of all our high-quality books, call toll free 1-800-542-2595 or fax 1-877-542-2596.

Library of Congress Cataloging-in-Publication Data

O'Mara, Jean Claude.
Raccoons in the dark / Jean Claude O'Mara.
    p. cm. — (Creatures of the night)
Includes index.
ISBN 978-1-4339-6378-0 (pbk.)
ISBN 978-1-4339-6379-7 (6-pack)
ISBN 978-1-4339-6376-6 (library binding) –
1. Raccoon—Juvenile literature. 2. Nocturnal animals—Juvenile literature. I. Title.
QL737.C26O63 2012
599.76'32—dc23

                                        2011033649

First Edition

Published in 2013 by
Gareth Stevens Publishing
111 East 14th Street, Suite 349
New York, NY 10003

Copyright © 2013 Gareth Stevens Publishing

Designer: Daniel Hosek
Editor: Therese Shea

Photo credits: Cover, p. 1 Rich Reid/National Geographic/Getty Images; p. 5 Masterfile.com; pp. 7, 9, 15, 19 Shutterstock.com; pp. 11, 17 Thinkstock.com; pp. 13, 21 iStockphoto.com.

Printed in the United States of America

CPSIA compliance information: Batch #CW12GS: For further information contact Gareth Stevens, New York, New York at 1-800-542-2595.

Contents

Boldface words appear in the glossary.

Nature's Burglars!

Crash! Have you ever heard a trash can tip over at night? A raccoon was probably looking for a snack. These animals like to be any place where they can find food. Since raccoons are active at night, they look like they're **sneaking** around!

Raccoons have interesting faces. They look as if they're wearing a black mask—like a burglar! Their bodies are often grayish. They may have black and brown fur as well. A raccoon's bushy tail has many black rings.

Kinds of Raccoons

There are two main kinds of raccoons. Northern raccoons live in Canada, the United States, and Central America. The crab-eating raccoon lives in Central and South America. There are some kinds of raccoons that live on islands.

Good with Their Hands

Raccoons have five long toes on each front paw. They use their paws like we use our hands. They can pick apart food if they need to. They eat mice, frogs, bugs, eggs, fish, plants, fruits, nuts, seeds, and much, much more!

11

Raccoons sometimes **dunk** their food in water. People used to think raccoons were washing their food when they did this. Now they think raccoons are just using the same actions they would if they were taking a fish from water.

Raccoons' sharp claws help them climb. They build dens in trees and logs. They like to use old nests and dens of other animals, too. Raccoons in towns and cities may make homes in buildings. All raccoons like to be near water.

Raccoons in Winter

Northern raccoons eat a lot in the fall. They need to get fat because they like to sleep through much of the winter. However, they may come out of their dens to hunt on warm winter days. Raccoons in warmer places are active all year round.

Raccoon Babies

A mother raccoon can have as many as seven babies—called cubs or kits—at a time. Raccoon cubs don't have a mask or rings on their tail at first. Their mother guards them. She doesn't even let the father near! She teaches her cubs how to find food.

Raccoon Enemies

Raccoons have a few **predators**. Foxes, owls, and eagles eat raccoon cubs. Raccoons can **protect** themselves. They're very fast runners. If caught, they'll fight. Raccoons also have good eyesight and hearing in the dark. These help them stay safe at night.

The Raccoon Fact Box

Length	24 to 42 inches (61 to 107 cm), including tail
Weight	8 to 20 pounds (3.6 to 9 kg)
Fun Fact	Part of the raccoon's scientific name comes from a Latin word meaning "laundryman" or "washer."
Life Span	2 to 3 years in the wild

Glossary

dunk: to dip into a liquid

predator: an animal that hunts other animals for food

protect: to guard

sneak: to act in a quiet way so that no one will hear or see

For More Information

Books

Landau, Elaine. *Raccoons: Scavengers of the Night*. Berkeley Heights, NJ: Enslow Publishers, 2006.

Owen, Ruth. *Raccoon Cubs*. New York, NY: Bearport Publishing, 2011.

Ripple, William John. *Raccoons*. Mankato, MN: Pebble Books, 2006.

Websites

Raccoon

animals.nationalgeographic.com/animals/mammals/raccoon/
Hear what a raccoon sounds like and read more facts about them.

Raccoon

dnr.wi.gov/org/caer/ce/eek/critter/mammal/raccoon.htm
Read about raccoon tracks and how to spot them.

Index